Yuletide Treasures

20 Christmas Miniatures for Solo Piano

Arranged by
Jolene Boyd

Lillenas PUBLISHING COMPANY

KANSAS CITY, MO 64141

CONTENTS

Joy to the World

A Mixolydian Adventure

G. F. HANDEL
Arr. by Jolene Boyd

O Come, All Ye Faithful

From Wade's "Cantus Diversi," 18th Century
Arr. by Jolene Boyd

God Rest Ye Merry, Gentlemen

English Melody, 18th Century
Arr. by Jolene Boyd

Angels We Have Heard on High

Traditional French Melody
Arr. by Jolene Boyd

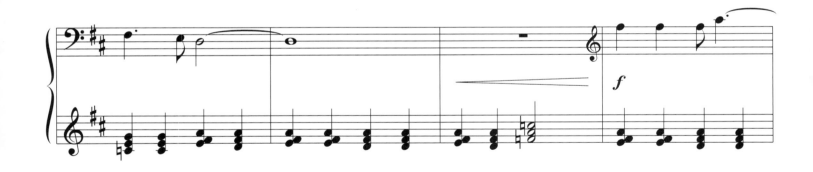

It Came upon the Midnight Clear

RICHARD S. WILLIS
Arr. by Jolene Boyd

O Come, Little Children

J. A. P. SCHULZ
Arr. by Jolene Boyd

Silent Night

FRANZ GRÜBER
Arr. by Jolene Boyd

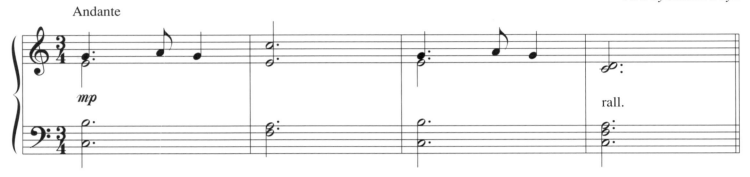

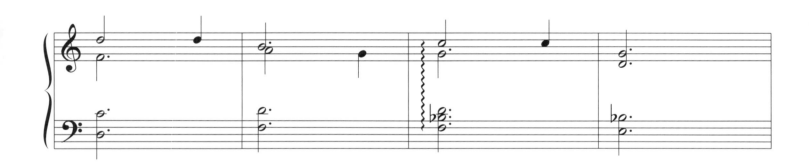

Jingle Bell Lullaby

(Jingle Bells)

JAMES PIERPONT
Arr. by Jolene Boyd

Here We Come A-Caroling

(The Wassail Song)

Traditional English Melody
Arr. by Jolene Boyd

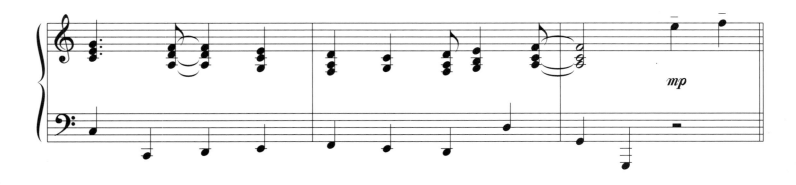

21

O Christmas Tree

Traditional German Melody
Arr. by Jolene Boyd

We Three Kings

JOHN H. HOPKINS, Jr.
Arr. by Jolene Boyd

Deck the Halls

Old Welsh Air
Arr. by Jolene Boyd

Optional: both hands 8va to the end

What Child Is This?

Traditional English Melody
Arr. by Jolene Boyd

O Come, O Come, Emmanuel

Plainsong, adapt. by THOMAS HELMORE
Arr. by Jolene Boyd

O Little Town of Bethlehem

LEWIS H. REDNER
Arr. by Jolene Boyd

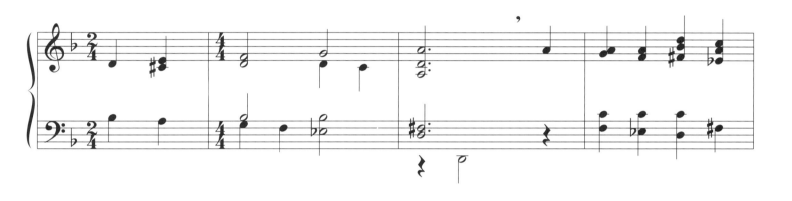

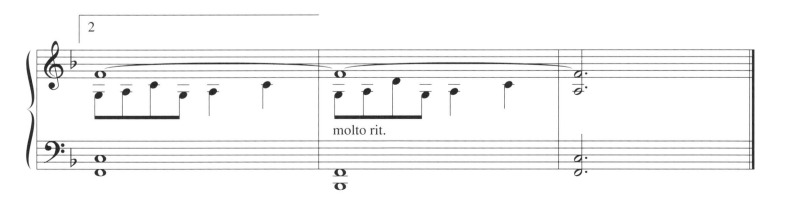

The First Noel

W. Sandys' *Christmas Carols*, 1833
Arr. by Jolene Boyd

Hark! the Herald Angels Sing

FELIX MENDELSSOHN
Arr. by Jolene Boyd

Away in a Manger

WILLIAM J. KIRKPATRICK
Arr. by Jolene Boyd

Angels from the Realms of Glory

HENRY SMART
Arr. by Jolene Boyd

While Shepherds Watched Their Flocks

GEORGE F. HANDEL
Arr. by Jolene Boyd